FAMOUS INVENTORS

LEGENDS AND GAME CHANGERS

BY MELISSA ROSS

eureka!

Eureka! books turn real stories into unforgettable experiences. This nonfiction imprint sparks curiosity, encourages critical thinking, and engages middle-grade readers. *Eureka!* books empower young minds to explore the stories of the real world, one fascinating fact at a time. Unravel the power of knowledge and lifelong learning with *Eureka!*

This edition first published in 2026 by Bellwether Media, Inc.

Library of Congress Cataloging-in-Publication Data

LC record for Famous Inventors available at: https://lccn.loc.gov/2025021805

Editor: Betsy Rathburn Series Designer: Jeffrey Kollock Book Designer: Josh Brink

Printed in the United States of America, North Mankato, MN.

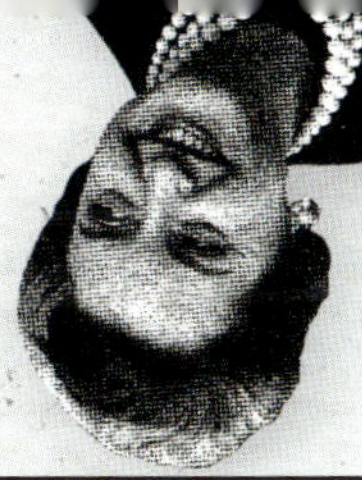

TABLE OF CONTENTS

INVENTION HISTORY

Inventions are machines or processes created to help people do something in a new way. Every invention starts with an idea that inspires an inventor to experiment and test, working to bring their vision into reality. Inventors seek to create something new that solves problems and makes life easier.

Around 3500 BCE, the invention of the wheel changed everyday life dramatically. It made work easier and travel faster. As centuries passed, new inventions such as the automobile and the airplane made travel even faster. Communication has benefited from invention, too. Movable type was invented around 1040 CE, leading to the printing press in the 1400s. News began to travel more quickly. Communication became even easier in 1876 with Alexander Graham Bell's telephone.

A whole new world of technology was born in 1975. The first successful personal computer, the Altair 8800, was released. In 1989, the World Wide Web connected people across the globe. In 2006, Chuck Hull's **3D printing** invention became available at home. **Artificial intelligence** (AI) continues to transform everyday life. The world of invention is full of endless possibilities!

TIMELINE

AROUND 3500 BCE
the wheel is invented in Mesopotamia

AROUND 1040 CE
Bi Sheng invents movable type

1400s
Johannes Gutenberg invents the printing press

1876 Alexander Graham Bell's telephone design is patented in the U.S.

1886 a vehicle built by Karl Benz is the first gas-powered car driven in public

1903 the Wright brothers make the first sustained and controlled flight

1913 Fred W. Wolf Jr. invents the first electric home refrigerator

1975 the Altair 8800 is released, becoming the first successful personal computer

1989 Tim Berners-Lee invents the World Wide Web

2006 the first 3D printer for home use is released

2020s many people begin using AI in everyday life

TECHNOLOGY

Technology lets people communicate more easily. In the 1830s, Charles Babbage designed the first digital computer. The first personal computers were available by the 1970s. Today, many computers use AI to solve problems and make decisions.

HEALTH AND SAFETY

Inventions have helped improve health and safety. In 1895, the discovery of X-rays led to the first X-ray machines. In the 1970s, new products made with Kevlar led to safer armor for people in dangerous jobs.

FOOD AND DRINK

Many inventors focus on creating new foods and drinks. From the chocolate chip cookie invented in the 1930s to the Cronut invented in the 2010s, these inventions help our world taste better.

COMMUNICATIONS

For many centuries, people have looked for faster ways to communicate. By the late 1800s, the earliest telephones let people communicate faster than ever before. Today, the internet lets people reach one another even more quickly.

MORE INVENTIONS, MORE INVENTORS!

DAILY LIFE

Daily life inventions are those that make everyday life more comfortable or fun. In the early 1900s, the airplane led to easier travel than ever before. Around the same time, the invention of plastic led to many new products.

TOYS AND GAMES

As people look for entertainment, inventors step up to create new products. Early video games took hold in the 1970s. Other toys take us outside. The Super Soaker was invented in the 1980s. Toys and games make life more fun!

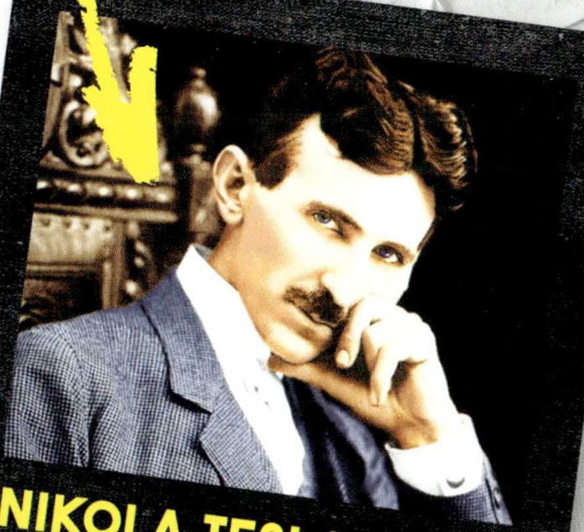

NIKOLA TESLA

Nikola Tesla was a Serbian-American engineer. He pioneered work in the area of radio invention in the late 1890s. This included the use of circuits to transmit radio waves. He invented the alternating current (AC) motor and power system. This invention made it possible to dispense power over longer distances, such as providing electricity to entire cities.

GEORGE DE MESTRAL

George de Mestral was a Swiss electrical engineer. In the 1940s, he invented hook-and-loop fasteners and named the invention Velcro. He got the idea from burrs stuck on his dog's fur after a walk. Today, Velcro is found on shoes, clothing, and even astronaut space suits.

LOUIS BRAILLE

Louis Braille was a French educator. He was also blind. In 1824, he invented a writing system called Braille. Blind people can learn the system and touch a series of raised dots to read. Braille is used by millions of people all over the world.

RUTH GRAVES WAKEFIELD

Ruth Graves Wakefield and her husband owned the Toll House Inn in Massachusetts. She invented the chocolate chip cookie in the 1930s and called it the Toll House Chocolate Crunch Cookie. Today, it is one of the most popular cookie flavors in the world.

TECHNOLOGY INVENTORS

Steve Wozniak is famous for being one of Apple's founders. He invented what many consider to be the first true personal computer.

Steve Wozniak

AN EARLY START

When he was young, Wozniak was fascinated by electronics. He built his first computer at age 13. After high school, Wozniak attended college for a short time. But he left to work at Hewlett-Packard (HP) in 1975.

FIRST APPLE

Around this time, the Altair 8800 personal computer kit was popular. Wozniak could not afford to buy a kit. Instead, he got the parts to build a computer himself. It became the Apple I. Unlike other personal computers of the time, the Apple I came fully assembled. Wozniak and Steve Jobs created a company to sell the computer.

> "My goal wasn't to make a ton of money. It was to build good computers."
> —Steve Wozniak

APPLE I REPLICA

MORE SUCCESS

Soon, Wozniak set to work designing the Apple II. It came out in 1977. It improved on the Apple I, making the personal computer more user-friendly. New software made the Apple II a popular computer for schools and businesses. Wozniak changed the world of personal computers. He also helped make Apple one of the world's top businesses.

APPLE II

OUTSIDE OF APPLE

Wozniak left Apple in 1985. In 1987, he released the CORE, a remote control that could be programmed to work with multiple devices. In 2002, he created Wheels of Zeus. This business created tags to help track items using **GPS**.

AWARDS AND HONORS

- **1979** Grace Murray Hopper Award
- **1985** National Medal of Technology
- **2000** National Inventors Hall of Fame
- **2014** Hoover Medal

BORN: August 11, 1950, in San Jose, California

EDUCATION: University of Colorado Boulder; De Anza College; University of California, Berkeley

KNOWN FOR: designed the Apple I and II personal computers

TIMELINE

- **1963** builds his first computer at age 13
- **1976** builds the Apple I personal computer and starts Apple with Steve Jobs
- **1977** builds the Apple II computer
- **1987** releases CORE, the first programmable universal remote control
- **2002** starts the company Wheels of Zeus

Chuck Hull invented 3D printing. His groundbreaking invention changed the world of product manufacturing. It has led to advances in medical devices, computer parts, space flights, and more.

Chuck Hull

STARTING OUT

Hull was born in Clifton, Colorado. In 1961, he earned an engineering physics degree from the University of Colorado Boulder. Afterward, he moved to California to start his career.

A SLOW PROCESS

In the early 1980s, Hull worked for a company that made plastic products using **ultraviolet** (UV) lamps. It was a slow process. Engineers often had to wait weeks for **prototypes** to be created to test their designs.

AWARDS AND HONORS

- **2014** National Inventors Hall of Fame
- **2020** Royal Photographic Society Progress Medal
- **2023** National Medal of Technology and Innovation

A PRINTED BOAT!

In 2019, a boat was made in only 70 hours by a huge 3D printer. The boat is 25 feet (7.6 meters) long!

TIMELINE

- **1961** graduates from the University of Colorado Boulder with an engineering physics degree
- **1983** prints the first object using 3D printing

SOLVING THE PROBLEM

Hull had an idea for a faster process. He used UV lamps to harden layers of plastic. The layers built up to form different shapes. In 1983, Hull finished his first successful object. It was a small plastic cup. The following year, he **patented** his process. He called it stereolithography. Today, it is called 3D printing.

PRINT IT OUT

In 1986, he started his own company, 3D Systems. It sold 3D-printed parts. It also sold 3D printers. The first commercial 3D printer was introduced in 1987.

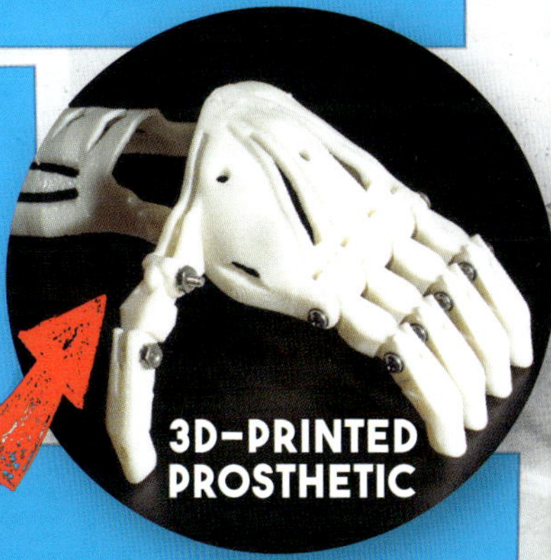

3D-PRINTED PROSTHETIC

MANY USES

Hull's invention has made the production of items faster and less expensive. It has proven especially valuable in the medical field. Anatomy models, medical devices, and **prosthetic** limbs are a few examples of products made using 3D printing.

CLIFTON

BORN: May 12, 1939, in Clifton, Colorado

EDUCATION: University of Colorado Boulder

KNOWN FOR: invented 3D printing and cofounded 3D Systems

1984 receives a patent for his 3D printing invention

1986 cofounds 3D Systems to manufacture 3D printers

1987 introduces the first 3D printer, SLA-1

George Carruthers

George Carruthers was an engineer and physicist whose inventions helped make new discoveries in space. His work helped increase our understanding of space.

TIMELINE

1964
begins working for the Naval Research Laboratory in Washington, D.C.

1969
the Far Ultraviolet Electrographic Camera is patented

1972
the Apollo 16 mission places the Far Ultraviolet Electrographic Camera on the moon

1986
an image of Halley's Comet is captured using Carruthers's instrument

1991
the STS-39 mission carries one of Carruthers's instruments to space

LOOKING TO THE STARS

As a kid, Carruthers enjoyed reading about space. By age 10, he had built his first telescope. His family moved to Chicago in 1952. In high school, Carruthers won awards in science fairs. He earned a degree in physics in 1961. He earned a doctorate in **aeronautical engineering** in 1964 and began working at the United States Naval Research Laboratory.

BORN: October 1, 1939, in Cincinnati, Ohio

DIED: December 26, 2020

EDUCATION: University of Illinois Urbana-Champaign

KNOWN FOR: invented the Far Ultraviolet Electrographic Camera

UNCOVERING HIDDEN SPACE

In 1969, Carruthers received a patent for his first invention. The Far Ultraviolet Electrographic Camera used UV light to take images of objects in space. The camera went to the moon in 1972. It took about 200 photos of newly discovered stars and galaxies. The camera was part of the first astronomy observatory on the moon. It is still there today!

MORE INVENTIONS

Carruthers invented other instruments used to study space. In 1986, one captured UV photos of Halley's Comet. In 1991, another instrument went to space on the STS-39 space shuttle mission. It carried two UV cameras.

EDUCATING OTHERS

Outside of inventing, George Carruthers helped develop the Science and Engineering **Apprenticeship** Program. The program allows high school students to work with scientists at the Naval Research Laboratory.

AWARDS AND HONORS

- **1972** NASA Exceptional Scientific Achievement medal
- **2003** National Inventors Hall of Fame
- **2011** National Medal of Technology and Innovation

HEALTH AND SAFETY INVENTORS

Gitanjali Rao is a young innovator and inventor. Named the *TIME* Kid of the Year in 2020, she has invented several devices that improve people's health.

> "Do not give up, and always remember the bigger goal of making a difference."
> — Gitanjali Rao

Gitanjali Rao

BORN: November 19, 2005, in Lone Tree, Colorado

EDUCATION: MIT

KNOWN FOR: invented Tethys, Epione, and Kindly

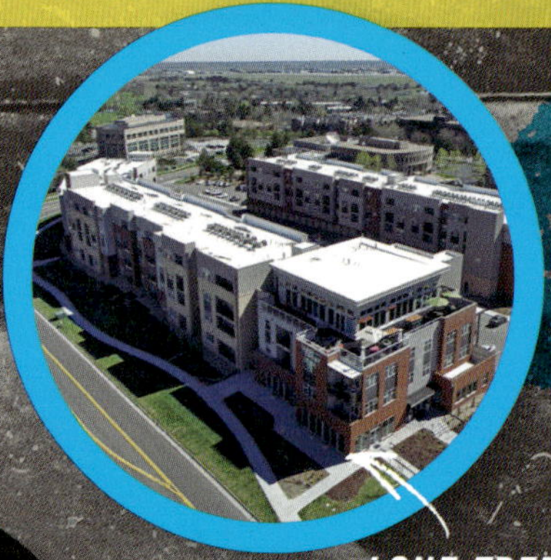

FIRST INVENTION

Rao was born in Lone Tree, Colorado. When she was around 4 years old, her uncle gave her a chemistry set that inspired her interest in STEM. When she was 10, she began working on a device to detect lead in drinking water. She named it Tethys. In 2017, she won a $25,000 prize for the invention. She received a patent for Tethys in 2021.

MORE SOLUTIONS

The next problem Rao tackled was addiction. In 2019, she invented Epione, a device that diagnoses addiction to some medications at an early stage. Epione looks at samples of proteins in people's bodies. It uses AI to compare them to other samples. Based on this comparison, it determines if the person is addicted.

STOP BULLYING

Rao worked with a team of fellow students to create a tool called Kindly. It uses AI that flags bullying language online. This helps teens recognize when they are not being nice to their peers.

INSPIRING OTHERS

Rao conducts workshops, inspiring young people to invent solutions to problems. In 2021, she was appointed as a UNICEF Youth Advocate. In 2023, she enrolled at the Massachusetts Institute of Technology (MIT).

AWARDS AND HONORS

- **2017** America's Top Young Scientist
- **2018** President's Environmental Youth Award
- **2020** *TIME* Kid of the Year
- **2022** Muhammad Ali Humanitarian Award

TIMELINE

- **2015** begins working on her Tethys invention
- **2017** wins a $25,000 prize for Tethys
- **2019** creates Epione to help combat addiction
- **2021** receives the patent for Tethys
- **2023** enrolls at MIT

Stephanie Kwolek

TIMELINE

1946 receives a degree in chemistry and begins working at DuPont

1950 moves to Wilmington, Delaware, with DuPont's Pioneering Research Laboratory

1950s contributes to the development of spandex

1965 invents Kevlar

1986 retires from DuPont

Stephanie Kwolek is a chemist known for inventing Kevlar. This ultra-strong material has over 200 uses, including bulletproof vests and body armor.

EARLY LEARNING

Kwolek grew up in Pennsylvania. When she was young, Kwolek enjoyed exploring the woods with her father. She learned how to sew from her mother. She went on to study chemistry, earning a degree in 1946.

NEW MATERIALS

After college, Kwolek began working as a chemist. She worked at a company called DuPont. There, she helped create new materials. One, Kapton, has been used to make spacecraft and satellites. Kwolek also contributed to the creation of spandex. This stretchy material is still used in clothing today.

INVENTING KEVLAR

In the 1960s, Kwolek was assigned to find a way to create strong but lightweight **synthetic** fibers. She experimented with different **polymers**, observing how they reacted to different conditions. During one experiment, the polymer she mixed formed a strong, stiff fiber. She had invented a new material! It was later named Kevlar. Kevlar was first sold in 1971. It has been used to make armor, car parts, clothing, musical instruments, and more.

KEVLAR FIBERS

SUPER STRENGTH

Kwolek invented Kevlar while trying to design a strong, lightweight tire material. Kevlar is heat resistant and five times stronger than steel.

AFTER RETIREMENT

Kwolek retired from DuPont in 1986. But she continued working in science. She served on committees for the National Academy of Sciences and the National Research Council. She earned many awards and was honored by numerous organizations.

BORN: July 31, 1923, in New Kensington, Pennsylvania

DIED: June 18, 2014

EDUCATION: Margaret Morrison Carnegie College

KNOWN FOR: invented Kevlar

AWARDS AND HONORS

- **1980** Chemical Pioneer Award
- **1995** National Inventors Hall of Fame
- **1996** National Medal of Technology and Innovation
- **1997** Perkin Medal

Patricia Bath

Patricia Bath was an **ophthalmologist** who invented the Laserphaco Probe, a device that safely removes **cataracts** from patients' eyes.

EARLY RESEARCH

Bath grew up in New York City. She excelled in high school and won a scholarship to a National Science Foundation summer program. There, she researched cancer cells. Her findings earned recognition from many people in the medical field. She graduated with a medical degree from Howard University in 1968.

CREATING COMMUNITY

Bath began working as an intern at Harlem Hospital. She noticed that many Black Americans did not get good eye care. They were more likely to develop blindness and other eye problems. She created a community ophthalmology program to help people who could not afford eye care. Similar programs spread.

AWARDS AND HONORS

- **2001** American Medical Women's Association Hall of Fame
- **2013** Association of Black Women Physicians Lifetime Achievement Award
- **2018** New York Academy of Medicine John Stearns Medal

TIMELINE

- **1968** earns a medical degree from Howard University
- **1973** completes a residency in ophthalmology at New York University

AN IMPORTANT INVENTION

In 1974, Bath began working in California. She realized that laser technology would effectively remove cataracts. She began working on the idea in 1981. But technology was not advanced enough yet. She developed it for several years and finally finished the Laserphaco Probe in 1986. The device breaks up eye cataracts, making them easier for doctors to remove. Bath received the patent for the device in 1988. It has restored sight to millions of people!

HELPING MORE PEOPLE SEE

Bath cofounded the American Institute for the Prevention of Blindness in 1976. The organization helps people receive the eye care they need to prevent blindness.

BORN: November 4, 1942, in New York City, New York

DIED: May 30, 2019

EDUCATION: Hunter College, Howard University, Columbia University, New York University

KNOWN FOR: invented the Laserphaco Probe and developed community ophthalmology

1976 cofounds the American Institute for the Prevention of Blindness

1986 completes the invention of the Laserphaco Probe

1988 receives a patent for the Laserphaco Probe

FOOD INVENTORS

Dominique Ansel is a pastry chef. He achieved worldwide acclaim with his pastry invention, the Cronut.

Dominique Ansel

MAKING A CRONUT

Cronuts are made using a process called lamination. Dough is rolled and folded with butter many times to create layers. Next, it may be fried, rolled in sugar, filled, or topped with a glaze.

THE YOUNG COOK

Dominique Ansel grew up in Beauvais, France. At age 16, he got a job at a restaurant to help provide for his family. He also enrolled in a free culinary school. When he was 19, he left home to complete a year as a cook with the French military.

THE PASTRY CHEF

After his military service, Ansel returned to France to work in bakeries. Eventually, he began working at a Paris restaurant called Fauchon. He worked there for almost eight years. In 2006, he moved to New York City to work as an executive pastry chef. While he was there, the restaurant he worked for earned its third **Michelin Star**.

A NEW PASTRY

In 2011, Ansel opened his own bakery. Many considered it the best in the city. More success came in 2013. After months of development, Ansel released the Cronut. It is a flaky, layered pastry that is a cross between a donut and a croissant. Hundreds lined up outside the bakery to get a taste. *TIME* magazine named it one of the best inventions of 2013!

MORE INVENTIONS

Ansel opened more bakeries worldwide. He published his third cookbook in 2024. A few of his many pastry inventions are Frozen S'mores and the Chocolate Chip Cookie Shot.

AWARDS AND HONORS

- **2014** James Beard Award
- **2015** Ordre du Mérite Agricole award
- **2017** World's Best Pastry Chef

BORN: around 1977 in Beauvais, France

EDUCATION: culinary school in Beauvais

KNOWN FOR: invented the Cronut and many other pastries

BEAUVAIS

TIMELINE

1993 begins working at a local restaurant and enrolls in a free culinary school

1999 begins working at Fauchon in Paris, France

2006 moves to New York City to work as an executive pastry chef

2011 opens Dominique Ansel Bakery in New York City

2013 invents the Cronut

George Washington Carver

George Washington Carver was an inventor known for his work in agriculture. He famously invented over 300 different uses for peanuts!

THE PLANT LOVER

Carver was born in Missouri. He and his family were enslaved by a local farmer. Around age 11, Carver left the farm to attend school. He began working odd jobs and studying on his own. He especially liked studying plants. In 1896, he earned a master's degree from Iowa State Agricultural College. He became a director at Tuskegee Institute in Alabama.

PLANTING PEANUTS

Carver experimented with crops. After many years of growing cotton, the soil in the South was depleted. Carver noticed that many Black **sharecroppers** struggled. His research found that peanuts and sweet potatoes would help replenish the soil. Carver set out to create new products made with these crops so that farmers could earn more money.

HUNDREDS OF INVENTIONS

Carver invented more than 300 uses for peanuts. Besides new foods, he created dyes, paints, synthetic rubber, and more. The products gave people more reasons to buy peanuts and sweet potatoes. This meant the farmers who produced them could profit from the crops.

THE CARVER MONUMENT

In 1943, President Franklin D. Roosevelt established the George Washington Carver National Monument in Missouri.

TIMELINE

AROUND 1875 — moves to a new city to attend school

1890 — begins studying music and art at Simpson College in Iowa

AWARDS AND HONORS

1923	1977	1990
Spingarn Medal	Hall of Fame for Great Americans	National Inventors Hall of Fame

BORN: near Diamond, Missouri, around 1864

DIED: January 5, 1943

EDUCATION: Simpson College, Iowa State Agricultural College

KNOWN FOR: invented hundreds of products made from peanuts

CONTINUING RESEARCH

In 1940, Carver established the Carver Research Foundation at Tuskegee for continued agricultural research. Thanks to his work, Carver has been **inducted** into the Hall of Fame for Great Americans and the National Inventors Hall of Fame.

1894 becomes the first Black American to obtain a bachelor of science degree

1896 earns a master's degree and becomes director of agricultural research at Tuskegee Institute

1940 founds the Carver Research Foundation at Tuskegee Institute

COMMUNICATIONS INVENTORS

Tim Berners-Lee is a British computer scientist who invented the World Wide Web. His work changed the way people communicate, work, and more.

Tim Berners-Lee

A YOUNG INVENTOR

Berners-Lee grew up around electronics. He learned to use electronics to make devices to control his model trains. Later, he attended the University of Oxford to study physics. There, he built his first computer.

LAYING THE GROUNDWORK

In 1980, Berners-Lee began working at CERN in Switzerland. He worked on many projects. The data for the projects was stored in different places. They were not linked together. Frustrated, Berners-Lee created a **hypertext** program called Enquire. It linked different pieces of information together. It made accessing information easier. But few people used it.

WEAVING THE WEB

In 1989, Berners-Lee began building on Enquire. He proposed a hypertext system that would let people share information with anyone in the world. People would make their information available online. People could access it at any time. This system became known as the World Wide Web. Berners-Lee created a browser that let people use it. The World Wide Web is how people use the internet today!

CONTRIBUTING MORE

In 1994, Berners-Lee founded the World Wide Web Consortium. In 1999, he wrote *Weaving the Web*, a book about creating the World Wide Web. For his contributions, he was later knighted by Queen Elizabeth II and inducted into the Internet Hall of Fame.

BORN: June 8, 1955, in London, England

EDUCATION: University of Oxford

KNOWN FOR: invented the World Wide Web

AWARDS AND HONORS

- **2004** Knight Commander, Order of the British Empire
- **2006** Institute of Physics President's Medal
- **2012** Internet Hall of Fame

"The Web does not just connect machines; it connects people."
— Tim Berners-Lee

TIMELINE

- **1976** graduates from the University of Oxford with a degree in physics
- **1980** starts working at CERN
- **1989** begins working on a hypertext system known as the World Wide Web
- **1994** establishes the World Wide Web Consortium
- **2012** cofounds the Open Data Institute

John Logie Baird

John Logie Baird was a Scottish engineer. He invented the first working mechanical television and the first color television.

EARLY ENGINEERING

Born in 1888, Baird was a curious child. He invented a battery-operated telephone system to talk with neighborhood friends. He even built a **generator** to create electricity in his home. No one else in his area had electricity at the time. He went on to study electrical engineering before working as an engineer for a local electric company. He started several businesses with little success.

ALWAYS THE INVENTOR

In the early 1920s, Baird began building a television. He used items such as boxes and bicycle parts. In 1924, his device transmitted an image. It was the first successful mechanical television! It used a rotating disk to scan an image. The image was converted to an electrical signal and sent to a receiving disk. The image could be seen on a glass plate.

TIMELINE

EARLY 1920s makes his first TV using everyday items

1924 transmits the first images using a mechanical television

1926 demonstrates the televising of moving objects to Britain's Royal Institution

1928 introduces color television technology

AWARDS AND HONORS

2006 National Library of Scotland Scottish Hall of Fame

2014 Society of Motion Picture and Televison Engineers Honor Roll

2015 Scottish Engineering Hall of Fame

MAKING IMPROVEMENTS

After more improvements, Baird used his technology to transmit across the Atlantic Ocean in 1928. The following year, the British Broadcasting Company (BBC) began using Baird's technology.

THE FAMOUS ENGINEER

Baird was inducted into the Scottish Engineering Hall of Fame and the National Library of Scotland's Scottish Hall of Fame.

HELENSBURGH

BORN: August 13, 1888, in Helensburgh, Scotland

DIED: June 14, 1946

EDUCATION: Royal Technical College, University of Glasgow

KNOWN FOR: invented the first working mechanical television

NOT ALONE

Baird was not the only television pioneer. Philo Farnsworth invented the first electric television in 1927.

Alexander Graham Bell was a scientist, inventor, and teacher. He invented the first working telephone, revolutionizing long-distance communication.

Alexander Graham Bell

GROWING UP

Bell grew up in Scotland. His mother was almost completely deaf, and his father taught deaf people. As a teenager, Bell joined his father in his work. He started university in 1868 but left in 1870 when his family moved to Canada.

SENDING SIGNALS

Soon, Bell moved to Boston to teach at a school for the deaf. He also began working to improve **telegraph** communication. In 1874, he found a way to send multiple messages at once over telegraph wire. These messages took the form of electrical signals.

AWARDS AND HONORS

- **1880** Volta Prize
- **1902** Albert Medal
- **1914** IEEE Edison Medal

THE FIRST PHONE CALL

Bell placed the first phone call in 1876. In a test call, he said to his assistant Thomas Watson, "Mr. Watson, come here, I want to see you."

TIMELINE

- **1871** moves to Boston and begins to improve the telegraph
- **1876** receives the patent for his invention and makes the first successful phone call

SENDING SOUNDS

Next, Bell turned his attention to transmitting sounds. In 1875, he created a device that could transmit a musical note. He soon drew up plans for a device that would transmit voice. But it did not work yet. Still, the patent for the device was granted in March 1876. Three days later, Bell successfully transmitted a voice through wire. The telephone was born!

GRAPHOPHONE

MORE INVENTIONS

Bell continued inventing. He designed the Graphophone in 1885. It was used to record and play sounds such as music. His audiometer used different sounds to determine a person's quality of hearing. Bell also founded the Volta Bureau in 1887 to improve the lives of deaf people.

EDINBURGH

BORN: March 3, 1847, in Edinburgh, Scotland

DIED: August 2, 1922

EDUCATION: University College London

KNOWN FOR: invented the telephone

1877 founds the Bell Telephone Company

1886 receives a patent for his Graphophone invention

1887 founds the Volta Bureau, a library devoted to educating deaf people

DAILY LIFE INVENTORS

Orville and Wilbur Wright were American inventors and aviation pioneers. They designed and built the first powered airplane controlled by a pilot.

Orville and Wilbur Wright

BUSINESS OWNERS

Brothers Orville and Wilbur Wright spent most of their lives in Ohio. They had many business ventures. In 1889, they opened a printing shop, publishing several newspapers. In the early 1890s, they opened a bicycle shop.

PLANNING TO FLY

In the late 1800s, the brothers became interested in aviation. They realized that airplanes needed a way to be controlled by the pilot. The brothers used their mechanical skills to come up with a new airplane design. Starting in 1899, they experimented with designs for gliders. They tested the gliders on beaches in North Carolina.

FIRST FLIGHT

In 1903, Orville and Wilbur completed a new design. That December, they finally achieved their goal of powered, controlled flight. Their Flyer airplane made the first successful flight controlled by a pilot. The modern age of aviation was born!

BORN: April 16, 1867, in Millville, Indiana

DIED: May 30, 1912

KNOWN FOR: invented the first pilot-controlled airplane

FLYING INTO HISTORY

The brothers continued making improvements with newer models. In 1909, they created the world's first military plane. They opened the first civilian flying school in the U.S. in 1910. After Wilbur passed away, Orville continued leading their business until 1915. The Wright brothers have gone down in history as aviation pioneers.

BORN: August 19, 1871, in Dayton, Ohio

DIED: January 30, 1948

KNOWN FOR: invented the first pilot-controlled airplane

AWARDS AND HONORS

- 1909 Congressional Gold Medal
- 1917 Albert Medal
- 1975 National Inventors Hall of Fame

TIMELINE

- **1889** open printing shop
- **EARLY 1890s** open bike shop
- **1900** build and test their first glider
- **1903** complete the first controlled, powered flight in history
- **1909** complete the first airplane for the U.S. military

Leo Baekeland

Leo Baekeland was a chemist. He invented a kind of plastic called Bakelite. He is considered the founder of the modern plastic industry.

STARTING OUT

Baekeland grew up in Belgium. In 1880, he began studying at the University of Ghent. He went on to earn a doctorate from the university. He taught chemistry there until 1889, when he moved to the U.S.

A NEW PAPER

In the U.S., Baekeland started his own company. It sold his invention, a paper called Velox. Velox was a photographic paper used to create photo prints in artificial light. Eventually, Baekeland sold the rights to the paper for around $1 million.

HIS BIGGEST DISCOVERY

Next, Baekeland began working on a replacement for **shellac**. He experimented with different chemicals and processes. In 1907, his experiments led to a new discovery. Baekeland had created a new type of plastic. Bakelite was the first hard, moldable plastic that did not melt in high heat.

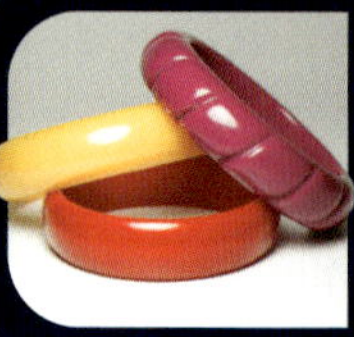

COLLECTOR'S ITEM

Many people collect Bakelite today. Bakelite jewelry is especially popular. Some pieces sell for hundreds of dollars!

TIMELINE

1889 moves from Belgium to the U.S.

1893 invents Velox paper, later selling the rights for around $1 million

BORN: November 14, 1863, in Ghent, Belgium

DIED: February 23, 1944

EDUCATION: University of Ghent

KNOWN FOR: invented Bakelite

GHENT

BAKELITE BUSINESS

In 1909, Baekeland was granted a patent for Bakelite. He started a company, Bakelite Corporation, to sell telephones, radios, jewelry, and other items made with the plastic. In 1939, Baekeland sold his business and retired. In time, more durable plastics were created. But Baekeland's early plastic invention makes him a plastics pioneer!

BAKELITE RADIO

AWARDS AND HONORS

- **1909** Nichols Medal of the Chemical Society
- **1913** Gibbs Medal
- **1916** Perkin Medal
- **1974** Plastics Hall of Fame

1907 invents Bakelite

1909 receives the patent for Bakelite and begins selling many plastic products

1939 retires from Bakelite Corporation

Frederick McKinley Jones was an inventor known as the "King of Cool." He held more than 60 patents in his lifetime. He is best known for inventing mobile refrigeration.

Frederick McKinley Jones

A YOUNG MECHANIC

From a young age, Jones had to rely on himself. By age 11, he began to work. Soon, he became interested in mechanics. In 1912, he moved to Minnesota to do mechanical work on a farm. He taught himself more about mechanics in his spare time. Eventually, he earned an engineering license.

ON TO THE ARMY

In 1918, Jones joined the Army to serve in World War I. His mechanical skills helped him quickly rise to the rank of sergeant. After the war, he worked to improve sound for the film industry. He invented a way to make silent movie projectors play movies with sound.

AWARDS AND HONORS

- **1944** American Society of Refrigeration Engineers
- **1991** National Medal of Technology
- **2007** National Inventors Hall of Fame

MOVIE TICKETS

In June 1939, Jones patented a machine that dispensed movie tickets. It was his first patent!

TIMELINE

- **1912** does mechanical work on a farm in Minnesota
- **1918** joins the Army to serve in World War I

KEEPING THINGS COOL

In 1938, Jones invented mobile refrigeration. His invention included a cooling device mounted under a truck trailer. It changed how people eat! The invention made it possible to transport **perishable** food long distances. Different types of produce were now available year-round.

SAVING LIVES

Jones soon cofounded the U.S. Thermo Control Company, now called Thermo King. The company's impact grew during World War II. Mobile refrigeration saved many soldiers' lives by transporting food, blood, and medicine. For his invention, Jones was the first Black American to receive the National Medal of Technology.

BORN: May 17, 1893, in Cincinnati, Ohio

DIED: February 21, 1961

KNOWN FOR: invented mobile refrigeration

LATE 1920s invents a way to convert silent movie projectors into sound projectors

1938 invents mobile refrigeration

MID-1950s retires from Thermo King

Thomas Edison

Thomas Edison is remembered as an inventor of many different devices. His most famous invention, the first practical **incandescent** light bulb, revolutionized daily life.

THE YOUNG LEARNER

At a young age, Edison lost most of his hearing. His mother educated him at home. He loved to read and learn. In 1859, he began selling newspapers at a railroad in Michigan. He soon got the opportunity to learn telegraphy. He studied ways to improve the technology.

ON TO INVENTING

In 1869, Edison left his job to devote himself to inventing. He invented the **phonograph** in 1877. It was the first device that could record and reproduce sound. In 1879, Edison completed his most famous invention. His light bulb contained a thin piece of **carbonized** thread. An electric current through the thread heated it to produce light. It was the first practical incandescent light bulb! It was safer and more affordable than other lights of the time.

AWARDS AND HONORS

- **1908** John Fritz Medal
- **1915** Franklin Medal in Engineering
- **1928** Congressional Gold Medal

LIGHTING UP THE CITY

Edison formed a company in 1880 to sell his light bulb. In 1882, Edison's company turned on the power at Pearl Street Station in New York City.

TIMELINE

- **1862** begins work as a telegrapher
- **1877** invents the phonograph

BORN: February 11, 1847, in Milan, Ohio

DIED: October 18, 1931

KNOWN FOR: invented the first practical incandescent light bulb

MILAN

KINETOSCOPE

MORE INVENTIONS

During his lifetime, Edison held 1,093 patents for inventions. A few of his devices include an electronic voting machine, a motion picture camera called a kinetoscope, and the first electric copy machine. He is one of the most famous inventors in the world.

1879 invents the first practical incandescent light bulb

1891 applies for a patent for the kinetoscope

AROUND 1910 invents a reliable alkaline battery

TOYS AND GAMES INVENTORS

Ralph Baer

Ralph Baer was an engineer and pioneer in the video game industry. He created the first home video game system.

ELECTRONIC BEGINNINGS

Baer was born to a Jewish family in Germany. When he was a teenager, he and his family fled to the U.S. to escape **persecution**. In 1940, he graduated from the National Radio Institute. He worked in radio electronics for several years. In 1949, he earned a degree in television engineering.

AN EARLY IDEA

In the early 1950s, Baer had an idea for a device that allowed people to play games on a TV. However, his supervisors did not see its value. In time, Baer got a new job at a company called Sanders Associates. His new supervisors liked his idea!

ENGINEERING THE IDEA

In 1967, Baer began working with a small team of engineers on his invention. By 1969, they had designed a box console with two controllers. Players used a joystick to play ping-pong, golf, handball, and other games. The device was known as the Brown Box. Sanders licensed it to a company called Magnavox. In 1972, they released it as the Magnavox Odyssey. The first home console was born!

MAGNAVOX ODYSSEY

MORE GAMES

In 1975, Baer started his own business to develop more electronic games and toys. The most popular was his Simon game, released in 1978. By the end of his career, Baer held over 150 patents.

BORN: March 8, 1922, in Rodalben, Germany

DIED: December 6, 2014

EDUCATION: National Radio Institute, American Television Institute of Technology

KNOWN FOR: invented the first home video game system

RODALBEN

AWARDS AND HONORS

- **2004** National Medal of Technology and Innovation
- **2010** National Inventors Hall of Fame
- **2014** IEEE Edison Medal

TIMELINE

- **1949** earns a degree in television engineering
- **1956** begins working for Sanders Associates
- **1967** starts working on the Brown Box prototype
- **1972** Magnavox releases Baer's design as the Magnavox Odyssey
- **1978** releases the Simon game
- **1987** retires from Sanders Associates

TIMELINE

- **1938** moves to California with her husband, Elliot Handler
- **1945** starts Mattel with Elliot and their business partner Harold Matson
- **1959** debuts Barbie at a toy fair
- **1976** founds Ruthton to develop prosthetics
- **2009** more than 1 billion Barbies sold since 1959

Ruth Handler

Ruth Handler is best known for inventing the Barbie doll. It is the world's best-selling doll.

YOUNG RUTH

When Handler was 6 months old, her mother became ill and could not care for her. Handler's sister and brother-in-law raised her in Colorado. She married Elliot Handler in 1938. They soon moved to California.

EARLY AMBITION

Handler was very ambitious. She encouraged Elliot to manufacture the furniture he designed. In 1945, the Handlers founded Mattel with their business partner, Harold Mattson. At first, the company made dollhouse furniture and picture frames. Eventually, it sold toys.

DENVER

COLORADO, USA

BORN: November 4, 1916, in Denver, Colorado

DIED: April 27, 2002

EDUCATION: University of Denver

KNOWN FOR: invented the Barbie doll and cofounded Mattel

INVENTOR

In the early 1950s, Handler's daughter enjoyed playing with paper dolls. She pretended her dolls were adults. This gave Handler the idea to make a new type of doll. She debuted the Barbie doll at a toy fair in 1959. Within a year, more than 300,000 Barbie dolls had sold. Today, more than 1 billion Barbie dolls have sold.

MORE ACCOMPLISHMENTS

Handler was diagnosed with cancer in 1970. She was inspired to help other survivors deal with the changes to their bodies after cancer. She invented a new type of prosthetic. In 1976, she founded a company called Ruthton to help sell them.

RUTH REMEMBERED

In 1967, Handler was named Woman of the Year in Business by the *Los Angeles Times*. She was inducted into the Toy Industry Hall of Fame in 1989.

AWARDS AND HONORS

1967
Los Angeles Times Woman of the Year in Business

1989
Toy Industry Hall of Fame (with Elliot)

1997
Global Business Hall of fame

ONE DOLL, MANY JOBS

Barbie is known for her many careers. Since 1959, the doll has had more than 200 different careers. These include doctor, astronaut, and Olympic skier.

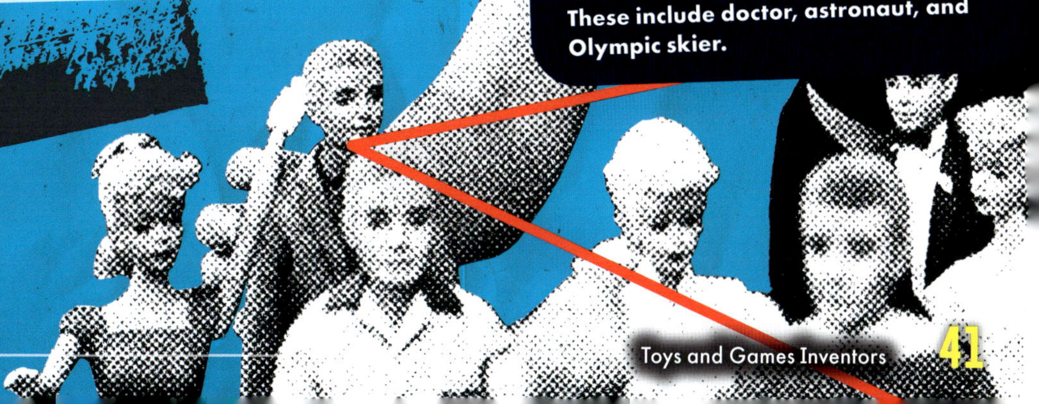

Lonnie Johnson

Engineer Lonnie Johnson is an inventor with several successful patents. He is most famous for the Super Soaker, a popular water gun toy.

A YOUNG ENGINEER

Johnson grew up in Alabama in the 1950s. When he was young, his father taught him how to make his own toys. Johnson represented his high school at a science fair. His remote-controlled robot, made from junkyard scraps, won first prize. He went on to earn a master's degree in **nuclear engineering** in 1975.

AWARDS AND HONORS

- **2011** State of Alabama Engineering Hall of Fame
- **2015** National Toy Hall of Fame
- **2022** National Inventors Hall of Fame

"...Perseverance and continuing to hone your skills is the key to being successful in anything you do."
—Lonnie Johnson

TIMELINE

- **1975** completes master's degree in nuclear engineering
- **1979** starts working at the NASA Jet Propulsion Laboratory

A NEW INVENTION

In 1979, he began working at the NASA Jet Propulsion Laboratory. He worked on NASA's missions to Mars and Jupiter. In his free time, he experimented with inventions. In 1982, he was working on a heat pump. He attached the nozzle to his bathroom sink. A stream of water shot out. Johnson quickly realized this could make a fun water gun toy for kids. It later became the Super Soaker. Today, more than 250 million Super Soakers have sold!

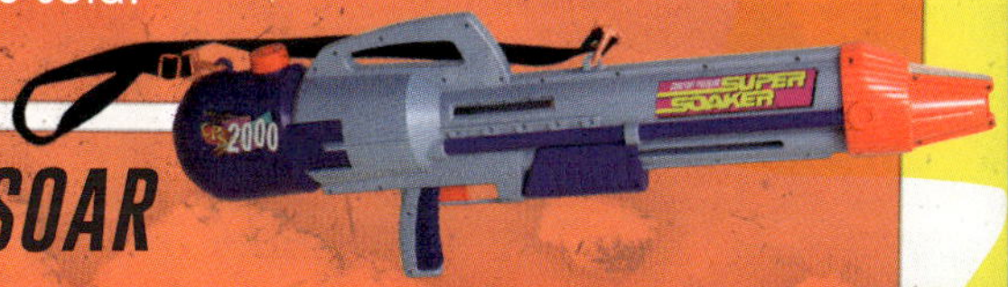

HIS INVENTIONS SOAR

Johnson holds more than 200 patents. In 2003, he invented a renewable energy system called the Johnson thermoelectric energy converter. Much of his work centers on methods of sustainable energy.

AWARD WINNER

The Super Soaker is still one of the most popular toys for kids. For the invention, Johnson was inducted into the National Inventors Hall of Fame in 2022.

BORN: October 6, 1949, in Mobile, Alabama

EDUCATION: Tuskegee Institute

KNOWN FOR: invented the Super Soaker

1982 creates the first prototype for the Super Soaker

1989 sells the Super Soaker to the Larami Corporation

2003 invents the Johnson thermoelectric energy converter

THE FUTURE OF INVENTIONS

The future of inventions is unlimited. Rapidly growing technologies like nanotechnology, robotics, and AI bring many possibilities. Future inventors may unlock new ways to use these technologies to solve problems, provide entertainment, and more!

MORE INVENTORS TODAY AND BEYOND

HANNAH HERBST

Hannah Herbst was a teenager when she invented BEACON. This device converts energy from ocean currents into electricity. Its purpose is to help provide electricity to people who live in developing nations. In 2015, Herbst was named America's Top Young Scientist because of the invention.

SHUBHAM BANERJEE

At age 13, Shubham Banerjee invented Braigo, a low-cost Braille printer made from LEGO bricks and small mechanical parts. Braigo's purpose is to print Braille from personal computers, making reading materials more accessible. The invention led Banerjee to found Brago Labs Inc.

ERIN SMITH

Erin Smith had an early interest in science. She did experiments in her kitchen. She was 16 years old when she invented FacePrint. It is a tool that records facial expressions to detect the early onset of Parkinson's disease.

XÓCHITL GUADALUPE CRUZ LÓPEZ

Xóchitl Guadalupe Cruz López comes from San Cristóbal de las Casas, Mexico. This community sometimes does not have hot water. People often have to take cold baths, even during cool weather. López was eight years old when she decided to do something about it. She invented a solar-powered water heater called Warm Bath. It can be made using affordable products, making it easy for many people to get.

HEMAN BEKELE

At age 14, Heman Bekele invented a bar of soap that treats skin cancer. He used nanotechnology with existing cancer-fighting chemicals to make the soap. In 2023, he won the 3M Young Scientist Challenge for the soap.

FIONN FERREIRA

From a young age, Fionn Ferreira enjoyed spending time in water. He also enjoyed learning about science. His interests led him to learn about harmful microplastics that are present in many bodies of water. He invented a method that uses a magnetic liquid to remove microplastics from water. It won the grand prize at the 2019 Google Science Fair.

GLOSSARY

3D printing—the process of making an object in which models are scanned and printed using many layers of materials stacked on top of one another

aeronautical engineering—a field of engineering that specializes in the development of aircraft

apprenticeship—a program in which a person learns a trade or occupation by training under an expert

artificial intelligence—a computer's ability to do things that a human mind can do

carbonized—converted into carbon or charcoal by heating or burning

cataracts—areas of the eye that are clouded, causing blurred vision

generator—a machine that converts energy into electricity

GPS—short for global positioning system; GPS is a navigational system that uses satellites to determine locations on Earth.

hypertext—a system that links topics on the screen to related information

incandescent—releasing light after being heated up

inducted—added

Michelin Star—an award given to restaurants for exceptional food and service

nanotechnology—the study of matter at a very small scale; nanotechnology is used to create new materials and devices.

nuclear engineering—a field of engineering that specializes in using nuclear energy to benefit people

ophthalmologist—a doctor who specializes in treating diseases that affect eyes

patented—protected with a document that gives an inventor all rights to create and sell their invention

perishable—likely to go bad quickly

persecution—cruel and unfair treatment, especially toward those who differ in religion, race, or beliefs

phonograph—an instrument that reproduces sound recorded on a grooved disk

polymers—substances made of large molecules that are made up of many repeating parts called monomers

prosthetic—related to human-made devices that replace or improve missing or injured body parts

prototypes—original or first models of something from which other forms are copied or developed

sharecroppers—farmers who work someone else's land and pay rent on the land with proceeds from the crops they grow

shellac—a substance made from lac bugs that is used as a final coating on some products

synthetic—something that is made by people using chemicals

telegraph—a device that sends messages at a distance through coded signals

ultraviolet—related to a kind of invisible light that is used in many industries such as medicine, water treatment, and manufacturing

WRITE ABOUT IT!

- What is something you would like to invent? **What would you need to make it?**

- Of all of the inventions in the book, **which one do you think changed the world the most?**

- Which one of the inventors would you like to learn more about? **Why?**

ALSO CHECK OUT

INDEX

The images in this book are reproduced through the courtesy of: Science History Institute, Harry Kalish./ Wikimedia Commons, front cover (Kwolek), p. 17 (Kwolek main photo); Open Data Institute Knowledge for Everyone/ Wikimedia Commons, front cover (Kwolek); Library of Congress/ Wikimedia Commons, front cover (Orville Wright), pp. 31 (Wilbur, Orville), 37 (Edison main); Thomas S England/ Getty Images, pp. 3 (Johnson), 42 (Johnson main); Los Angeles Times Photographic Collection/ Wikimeida Commons, p. 3 (Handler); Harris & Ewing/ Wikimedia Commons, p. 3 (GRAHAM BELL); pressmaster, pp. 4-5 (main photo); Amfeli/ Wikimedia Commons, p. 4 (1400s); Alonso de Mendoza/ Wikimedia Commons, p. 5 (1886); John T. Daniels/ Wikimedia Commons, p. 5 (1903); tomislav medak/ Wikimedia Commons, p. 5 (1975); Hod Lipson/ Wikimedia Commons, p. 5 (2006); Stock 4you, p. 5 (2020s); Peter Häll/ Wikimedia Commons, p. 6 (computer); pulsepowernow.com/ Wikimedia Commons, p. 7 (Tesla); Pictorial Press/ Alamy Stock Photo, pp. 7 (Mestral), 17 (Kwolek small photo), 27 (Baird profile); Popperfoto/ Getty Images, p. 7 Louis Braille; Theo's Little Bot/ Wikimedia Commons, p. 7 (Wakefield); Gage Skidmore/ Wikimedia Commons, pp. 8 (Wozniak small photo), 9 (Wozniak profile); Nichollas Harrison/ Wikimedia Commons, p. 8 (Wozniak main photo); Andrew Sozinov, p. 8 (Apple I replica); Rama & Musée Bolo/ Wikimedia Commons, p. 9 (Apple II); Rob Janoff/ Wikimedia Commons, p. 9 (Apple logo); Dreamframer, p. 9 (San Jose); UPI/ Alamy Stock Photo, p. 10 (Hull); Photo Researchers/ Alamy Stock Photo, pp. 11 (prosthetic), 33 (Baekeland main); picture alliance/ Getty Images, p. 11 (Hull profile); Jeffrey Beall/ Wikimedia Commons, p. 11 (Clifton Colorado); NASA on The Commons/ Wikimedia Commons, p. 12 (Carruthers small photo); U.S. Naval Research Laboratory/ Wikimedia Commons, p. 12 (Carruthers profile); Richard, pp. 12 (Cincinnati), 35 (Cincinnati); Mark Grant/ Wikimedia Commons, p. 13 (launch pad for STS-39); Charles Dharapak/ AP Images, p. 13 (Carruthers main); Eugene Gologursky/ Getty Images, p. 14 (Rao); Rachel Murray/ Getty Images, p. 14 (Rao profile); Dale, p. 14 (lone tree); Industriemuseum Gent/ Wikimedia Commons, p. 16 (Kevlar Fibers); Doug Kerr, p. 17 (New Kensington); HAGLEY MUSEUM AND ARCHIVE/ ScienceSourceImages, p. 17 (Kwolek profile); National Library of Medicine/ Wikimedia Commons, p. 18 (Bath small photo); Jemal Countess/ Getty Images, pp. 18 (Bath main photo), 19 (Bath profile); Tierney, p. 19 (New York City); Ari Perilstein/ Getty Images, p. 20 (Ansel main); Evan-Amos/ Wikimedia Commons, pp. 21 (Croissant-Donut), 38 (Magnavox Odyssey); Brent Herrig/ Wikimedia Commons, p. 21 (Ansel profile); guitou60, p. 21 (Beauvais); RuggyBearLA/ Wikimedia Commons, p. 22 (Carver monument); Universal History Archive/ Getty Images, pp. 22-23 (Carver main); Danita Delimont, p. 23 (Diamond, Missouri); Gado/ Getty Images, p. 23 (Carver profile); khumthong, p. 23 (peanuts); Rita Franca/ AP Newsroom, p. 24 (Berners-Lee main); Sven Braun/ AP Newsroom, p. 24 (Berners-Lee small); Oliver Berg/ AP Newsroom, p. 25 (Berners-Lee profile); Photocreo Bednarek, p. 25 (London); Orrin Dunlap, Jr./ Wikimedia Commons, p. 26 (Baird); Mr.Nostalgic/ Wikimedia Commons, p. 27 (Baird small); Thomas, p. 27 (Helensburgh); Opencooper/ Wikimedia Commons, p. 27 (Baird main); American Photo Archive/ Alamy Stock Photo, p. 28 (Bell small); Harris & Ewing, photographer/ Wikimedia Commons, p. 28 (Bell main); Crawdad Blues/ Wikimedia Commons, p. 29 (graphophone); Arcady, p. 29 (Edinburgh); ArtMechanic/ Wikimedia Commons, p. 29 (Bell profile); Scewing/ Wikimedia Commons, p. 30 (Orville_Wilbur_Wright main); Donald Trung/ Wikimedia Commons, p. 30 (airplane); Paul Thomas Curry, p. 31 (Millville); Zenstratus, p. 31 (Dayton); Struthious Bandersnatch/ Wikimedia Commons, p. 32 (Baekeland small); Geertivp/ Wikimedia Commons, p. 32 (Baekeland); Cynthia, p. 32 (Bakelite jewelry); SPCOLLECTION/ Alamy Stock Photo, p. 33 (Baekeland profile); Boris Stroujko, p. 33 (Ghent); Sergio Schnitzler, p. 33 (Bakelite radio); CrutchDerm2014/ Wikimedia Commons, p. 34 (Jones statue); Star Tribune via Getty Images/ Getty Images, pp. 34 (Jones main), 35 (Jones profile); FlickreviewR/ Wikimedia Commons, p. 35 (Jones); U.S. National Park Service/ Wikimedia Commons, pp. 36 (Edison small, Edison middle), 37 (Edison profile, kinetoscope); Levin C. Handy/ Wikimedia Commons, p. 36 (Edison bottom); Chris Light/ Wikimedia Commons, p. 37 (Milan); Stefan Krempl/ WENN/ Newscom, p. 38 (Baer main); Michael Schilling/ Wikimedia Commons, p. 38 (Baer small); HarshLight/ Wikimedia Commons, p. 39 (Simon game); dpa picture alliance/ Alamy Stock Photo, p. 39 (Ralph Baer profile); Fotolyse, p. 39 (Rodalben); Paolo Bona, p. 40 (Barbie doll); f11photo, p. 40 (Denver); Jeff Christensen/ Getty Images, p. 40 (Handler profile); Mattel/ Wikimedia Commons, p. 41 (Barbie logo); Adam Cuerden/ Wikimedia Commons, p. 41 (Handler profile); Rayhe/ Wikimedia Commons, p. 43 (Super Soaker); SeanPavonePhoto, p. 43 (Mobile); JOHN BAZEMORE/ AP Newsroom, p. 43 (Johnson middle); Office of Naval Research/ Wikimedia Commons, p. 43 (Johnson profile); amorn, p. 44 (robotics); Tong Wu/ TNS/ Newscom, p. 44 (Herbst); David Paul Morris/ Getty Images, p. 44 (Banerjee); Lea Suzuki/ San Francisco Chronicle/ AP Newsroom, p. 45 (Smith); Ivan Stephens/ AP Newsroom, p. 45 (López); Photo/ Nick Wass/ AP Newsroom, p. 45 (Bekele); Andy Gibson/ Alamy Stock Photo, p. 45 (Ferreira).